Internet of Things (IOT): A
for Nigeria

Dr Alex Ndukwe

First printing, 2019

Printed in the united states of America

ISBN: 978-1-79481-457-8

Dedication

I dedicate this book to **Mrs Chika Amadife** for her efforts in building an ecommerce site, she has been a source of encouragement.

Forward

IOT is basically connection of devices across the internet with the sole aim of generating data that will aid effective decision making. It can be applied to various sector of the economy.

The book looks at Health care, Agriculture , banking and finance, public sector etc. challenges are often experienced when data is inaccurate , like agriculture waste can be eliminated , fertilizers can be applied accurately since the data of the soil is accurate.

This concept has been applied in Medicare in advanced countries and has yielded positive results, diagnosis which consumes all the time of patients have since been handled by connection of devices to check blood pressure , sugar level , temperature and heart related checks.

Internet penetration is a major challenge in Nigeria, this can only be improved, Nigeria is ranked 7th in the world for internet usage, question here is what purposes and the answer is very clear, uses for social media like Facebook, Instagram, Pinterest etc. Facebook has 139 million users; Instagram has 6.972 Million Users. Technology investors around the world see Nigeria as an emerging market.

IOT can thrive in Nigeria and the Telco's, regulators can make it happen in a shortest possible time.

The book is a must read for every technology savvy individual in Nigeria, opportunities are abound for creating IOT service firm that will drive this initiative especially in our health care system.

Alex Ndukwe

Table of Contents

Data flows through an organization like blood in the circulatory system, and each day, each hour there are a myriad...........

Overview of IOT

The Internet of Things is an emerging topic of technical, social, and economic significance. Consumer products, durable goods, cars and trucks, industrial and utility components, sensors, and other everyday objects are being combined with Internet connectivity and powerful data analytic capabilities that promise to transform the way we work, live, and play. It is projected that about100 billion connected IoT devices and a global economic impact of more than $11 trillion by 2025.

The term Internet of Things generally refers to scenarios where network connectivity and computing capability extends to objects, sensors and everyday items not normally considered computers, allowing these devices to generate, exchange and consume data with minimal human intervention. There is, however, no single, universal definition. Though it is not a new phenomenon for event, processes to be

Data flows through an organization like blood in the circulatory system, and each day, each hour there are a myriad...........

monitored by use of computer for example process control in a refinery where temperatures, pressures are monitored from computers, faults can be rectified and same applies to electricity companies that monitor their stations and substations from a computer. These have existed but without any economic values involved in the IOT today. These include Ubiquitous Connectivity, Widespread Adoption of IP-based Networking, Computing Economics, Miniaturization, Advances in Data Analytics, and the Rise of Cloud Computing. Four common communications models described by the Internet Architecture Board include: Device-to-Device, Device-to-Cloud, Device-to-Gateway, and Back-End Data-Sharing. These models highlight the flexibility in the ways that IoT devices can connect and provide value to the user.

The IOT concept has not been around for too long a time, However, there have been visions of machines communicating with one another since the early 1800s. Machines have been providing direct communications since the telegraph (the first landline) was developed in the 1830s and 1840s. Described as "wireless telegraphy," the first radio voice transmission took place on June 3, 1900, providing another necessary component for developing the Internet of Things.

The Internet, itself a significant component of the IoT, started out as part of DARPA (Défense Advanced Research Projects Agency) in 1962, and evolved into ARPANET in 1969. In the 1980s, commercial service providers began supporting public use of ARPANET, allowing it to evolve into our modern Internet. Global Positioning Satellites (GPS) became a reality in early 1993, with the Department of Défense providing a stable, highly functional system of 24 satellites. This was quickly followed by privately owned, commercial satellites being placed in orbit. Satellites and landlines provide basic communications for much of the IoT. Steve Leibson, of the Computer History Museum, states, "The address space expansion means that we could assign an IPV6 address to every atom on the surface of the earth, and still have enough addresses left to do another 100+ earths." Put another way, we are not going to run out of internet addresses anytime soon.

A classical example of an IOT existed in 1980 , Coca cola installed a refrigerator connected to the network at Carnegie Melon University , programmers connect by internet to the appliance to verify if a drink is available and if it is cold before proceeding to it's location, this was just an innovation to serve it's teeming customers.

IOT evolved officially in 2013 into system using multiple technologies, ranging from the Internet to wireless communication and from micro-electromechanical systems (MEMS) to embedded systems. The traditional fields of automation (including the automation of buildings and homes), wireless sensor networks, GPS, control systems, and others, all support the IoT.

There are five key issues that could impact on the effectiveness of this concept and they are as follows:

Data flows through an organization like blood in the circulatory system, and each day, each hour there are a myriad...........

(1) Security

(2) Privacy

(3) Interoperability and Standards

(4) Legal, Regulatory and rights

(5) Emerging economy and development issues

Security

Security is one of the greatest challenges is that the hackers could take advantage of vulnerability of these devices connected on the network, owners of these device must ensure that the environment is properly protected and the device in question is also fortified against such intrusion. IT security firms are also ensuring they protect such devices from attacks. Let's review the attacks on The Mirai Botnet (aka Dyn Attack) and The Hackable Cardiac Devices from St. Jude

1. The Mirai Botnet (aka Dyn Attack)

Back in October of 2016, the largest DDoS attack ever was launched on service provider Dyn using an IoT botnet. This led to huge portions of the internet going down, including Twitter, the Guardian, Netflix, Reddit, and CNN.

This IoT botnet was made possible by malware called Mirai. Once infected with Mirai, computers continually search the internet for vulnerable IoT devices and then use known default usernames and passwords to log in, infecting them with malware. These devices were things like digital cameras and DVR players.

2. The Hackable Cardiac Devices from St. Jude

Early last year, CNN wrote, "The FDA confirmed that St. Jude Medical's implantable cardiac devices have vulnerabilities that could allow a hacker to access a device. Once in, they could deplete the battery or administer incorrect pacing or shocks, the FDA said. The devices, like pacemakers and defibrillators, are used to monitor and control patients' heart functions and prevent heart attacks." The article continued to say, "The vulnerability occurred in the transmitter that reads the device's data and remotely shares it with physicians. The FDA said hackers could control a device by accessing its transmitter."

These are examples of vulnerabilities of devices hijacked and the advice is that manufacturer of devices needs to adhere to the advice given by PC world that states as follows:

- "Devices that cannot have their software, passwords, or firmware updated should never be implemented.

- Changing the default username and password should be mandatory for the installation of any device on the Internet.

- Passwords for IoT devices should be unique per device, especially when they are connected to the Internet.

- Always patch IoT devices with the latest software and firmware updates to mitigate vulnerabilities."

Data flows through an organization like blood in the circulatory system, and each day, each hour there are a myriad...........

This would improve the security of such devices. Most of us might wonder that money is not lost but the workability of the devices becomes doubtful when hacked because it would not generate the correct data required to take decisions like the st Jude example. Improvement of security must be a continual process, with devices having their firmware updated regularly with software patch.

Privacy

The full potential of the Internet of Things depends on strategies that respect individual privacy choices across a broad spectrum of expectations. The data streams and user specificity afforded by IoT devices can unlock incredible and unique value to IoT users but concerns about privacy and potential harms might hold back full adoption of the Internet of Things. This means that privacy rights and respect for user privacy expectations are integral to ensuring user trust and confidence in the Internet, connected devices, and related services.

Indeed, the Internet of Things is redefining the debate about privacy issues, as many implementations can dramatically change the ways personal data is collected, analysed, used, and protected. For example, IoT amplifies concerns about the potential for increased surveillance and tracking, difficulty in being able to opt out of certain data collection, and the strength of aggregating IoT data streams to paint detailed digital portraits of users. While these are important challenges, they are not insurmountable. In order to realize the opportunities, strategies will need to be developed to respect individual privacy choices across a broad spectrum of expectations, while still fostering innovation in new technology and services.

The most dangerous part of IoT is that consumers are surrendering their privacy, bit by bit, without realizing it, because they are unaware of what data is being collected and how it is being used. As mobile applications, wearables and other Wi-Fi-connected consumer products replace "dumb" devices on the market, consumers will not be able to buy products that don't have the ability to track them. It is normal for consumers to upgrade their appliances, and it most likely does not occur to them that those new devices will also be monitoring them.

Interoperability / Standards

A fragmented environment of proprietary IoT technical implementations will inhibit value for users and industry. While full interoperability across products and services is not always feasible or necessary, purchasers may be hesitant to buy IoT products and services if there is integration inflexibility, high ownership complexity, and concern over vendor lock-in. In addition, poorly designed and configured IoT devices may have negative consequences for the networking resources they connect to and the broader Internet.

Appropriate standards, reference models, and best practices also will help curb the proliferation of devices that may act in disrupted ways to the Internet. The use of generic, open, and widely available standards as technical building blocks for IoT devices and services (such as the Internet Protocol) will support greater user benefits, innovation, and economic opportunity.

Legal, Regulatory and Rights

The use of IoT devices raises many new regulatory and legal questions as well as amplifies existing legal issues around the Internet. The questions are wide in scope, and the rapid rate of change in IoT technology frequently outpaces the ability of the associated policy, legal, and regulatory structures to adapt.

One set of issues surrounds cross border data flows, which occur when IoT devices collect data about people in one jurisdiction and transmit it to another jurisdiction with different data protection laws for processing. Further, data collected by IoT devices is sometimes susceptible to misuse, potentially causing discriminatory outcomes for some users. Other legal issues with

IoT devices include the conflict between law enforcement surveillance and civil rights; data retention and destruction policies; and legal liability for unintended uses, security breaches or privacy lapses.

While the legal and regulatory challenges are broad and complex in scope, adopting the guiding Internet Society principles of promoting a user's ability to connect, speak, innovate, share, choose, and trust are core considerations for evolving IoT laws and regulations that enable user rights.

Emerging Economy and Development Issues

The Internet of Things holds significant promise for delivering social and economic benefits to emerging and developing economies. This includes areas such as sustainable agriculture, water quality and use, healthcare, industrialization, and environmental management, among others. As such, IoT holds promise as a tool in achieving the United Nations Sustainable Development Goals.

The broad scope of IoT challenges will not be unique to industrialized countries. Developing regions also will need to respond to realize the potential benefits of IoT. In addition, the unique needs and challenges of implementation in less-developed regions will need to be addressed, including infrastructure readiness, market and investment incentives, technical skill requirements, and policy resources.

The Internet of Things is happening now. It promises to offer a revolutionary, fully connected "smart" world as the relationships between objects, their environment, and people become more tightly intertwined. Yet the issues and challenges associated with IoT need to be considered and addressed for the potential benefits for individuals, society, and the economy to be realized.

Data flows through an organization like blood in the circulatory system, and each day, each hour there are a myriad..........

Ultimately, solutions for maximizing the benefits of the Internet of Things while minimizing the risks will not be found by engaging in a polarized debate that pits the promises of IoT against its possible perils. Rather, it will take informed engagement, dialogue, and collaboration across a range of stakeholders to plot the most effective ways forward.

Challenges of Internet Penetration

There is improvement in Nigeria with respect to internet usage and available statics reveals that Nigeria is ranked 7th in the world among top 20 countries, please look at the table in the next page:

Data flows through an organization like blood in the circulatory system, and each day, each hour there are a myriad...........

TOP 20 COUNTRIES WITH HIGHEST NUMBER OF INTERNET USERS - JUNE 30, 2019

#	Country or Region	Population, 2019 Est.	Population 2000 Est.	Internet Users 30 June 2019	Internet Users 31 Dec 2000	Internet Growth 2000 - 2019
1	China	1,420,062,022	1,283,198,970	829,000,000	22,500,000	3,584 %
2	India	1,368,737,513	1,053,050,912	560,000,000	5,000,000	11,100 %
3	United States	329,093,110	281,982,778	292,892,868	95,354,000	207 %
4	Brazil	212,392,717	175,287,587	149,057,635	5,000,000	2,881 %
5	Indonesia	269,536,482	211,540,429	143,260,000	2,000,000	7,063 %
6	Japan	126,854,745	127,533,934	118,626,672	47,080,000	152 %
7	Nigeria	200,962,417	122,352,009	119,506,430	200,000	59,653 %
8	Russia	143,895,551	146,396,514	109,552,842	3,100,000	3,434 %
9	Bangladesh	168,065,920	131,581,243	94,445,000	100,000	94,345 %
10	Mexico	132,328,035	101,719,673	88,000,000	2,712,400	3,144 %
11	Germany	82,438,639	81,487,757	79,127,551	24,000,000	229 %
12	Turkey	82,961,805	63,240,121	69,107,183	2,000,000	3,355 %
13	Philippines	108,106,310	77,991,569	67,000,000	2,000,000	3,250 %
14	Vietnam	97,429,061	80,285,562	64,000,000	200,000	31,900 %
15	United Kingdom	66,959,016	58,950,848	63,356,621	15,400,000	311 %
16	Iran	82,503,583	66,131,854	62,702,731	250,000	24,981 %
17	France	65,480,710	59,608,201	60,421,689	8,500,000	610 %
18	Thailand	69,306,160	62,958,021	57,000,000	2,300,000	2,378 %
19	Italy	59,216,525	57,293,721	54,798,299	13,200,000	315 %
20	Egypt	101,168,745	69,905,988	49,231,493	450,000	10,840 %
	TOP 20 Countries	5,187,499,066	4,312,497,691	3,131,087,014	251,346,400	1,145 %
	Rest of the World	2,528,724,143	1,832,509,298	1,291,407,608	109,639,092	1,077 %
	Total World	7,716,223,209	6,145,006,989	4,422,494,622	360,985,492	1,125 %

Source: miniwatts Marketing Group

Data flows through an organization like blood in the circulatory system, and each day, each hour there are a myriad...........

It is a different ball game when we consider internet penetration rate which is still very low at 8.5% , Nigeria is not among the top 25 countries with high penetration rates, how is this rate computed, The penetration rate is easy to calculate if you know your target market size. To calculate the penetration rate, divide the number of customers you have by the size of the target market and then multiply the result by 100. Connecting speed which determines the quality of connections experienced by users. The quality of internet service provided by the telecom operators in Nigeria is considered poor due to poor infrastructure in some states it is very difficult to achieve 4G connection.

Licenced ISP firms have taken a bold step to provide 4G wireless network which is at a very high cost for consumers and the reasons are not far fetched, cost of delivering these services coupled with cost of doing business in Nigeria, internet should not be luxury but a necessity that could propel our digital economy.

The use of internet is beyond just for browsing applications or social media like Facebook, Instagram etc. internet serves as connections of devices that would help alleviate the challenges of poor processes in healthcare, agriculture, oil and gas, Schools, banking and finance etc. we need to have a strong internet connection and reduced cost of connection before we can even think of an enhanced digital economy, FGN can subsidise duty on imported equipment by the ISP and this can lower the cost of connection for the teeming consumers. FIRS can collect tax on IOT Devices implemented in the country, but the advice is to make connections very reduced to encourage penetration and improve the quality of connections we would proceed on our journey to sustainable IOT implementation in Nigeria.

Data flows through an organization like blood in the circulatory system, and each day, each hour there are a myriad............

It will be a thing of Joy for us to transit from theory to practical, seminars and conferences have been delivered by consultants on the subject matter, but the grey areas remained unresolved as we continue to tell stories and its implementation remains a mirage.

IOT can boost revenue for FGN if we can improve on our infrastructure, reduce the cost of internet connection and improve quality, regulators are doing a good job by following the broadband plan for 2013 to 2018 by offering more licence for new ISP companies.

Chapter One

IOT in Manufacturing

Industrial Internet of Things (IIoT) is a way to digital transformation in manufacturing. Industrial IoT employs a network of sensors to collect critical production data and uses cloud software to turn this data into valuable insights about the efficiency of the manufacturing operations. This will eliminate trial by error that leads to waste of resources and efficiency.

The adoption drivers for the Industrial IoT solutions include:

Cost reduction.

Due to optimized asset and inventory management (hence, lower inventory carrying costs and search times), reduced machine downtime, more agile operations, and more efficient energy use, companies reduce operational costs and even create new sources of revenue (for instance, smart, connected products allow to shift from selling products to selling experience – product usage and post-sale services). McKinsey estimates that IoT applications in manufacturing are expected to generate $1.2 to $3.7 trillion of economic value annually by 2025.

Shorter time-to-market.

Faster and more efficient manufacturing and supply chain operations allow to significantly reduce product cycle time. Harley-Davidson, for instance, leveraged IoT to reconfigure its York, PA manufacturing facility and reduce the time it takes to produce a motorbike from a 21-day cycle to six hours.

Mass customization.

Mass customization allows businesses to create products tailored to the needs of a purchaser, while retaining high production volumes. The manufacturing process behind that requires a dramatic increase in the variety of produced SKUs. The increase in the number of SKUs (each requiring different

materials and components) causes inventory to go up and become more diverse. At the same time, manufacturing operations get more complex: the production of, say, 20 items of SKU X can be immediately followed by the production of 10 items of SKU Y. It makes monitoring the effectiveness of manufacturing operations and the location of inventory items burdensome and, in some cases, not feasible. IIoT facilitates mass customization by becoming a source of real-time data required for thoughtful forecasting, shop floor scheduling and routing.

Improved safety.

IIoT helps to ensure a safer workplace. Paired with wearable devices, IIoT allows monitoring workers' health state and risky activities that can lead to injuries. Along with ensuring workers' safety, IIoT addresses safety problems in potentially hazardous environments. For instance, in oil and gas industry, IIoT is applied to monitor gas leakages as it travels through the pipe network.

Product quality control based on condition monitoring

Monitoring the quality of the produced goods can be carried out in two ways: by inspecting a WIP (work in progress) as it moves through the production cycle or by monitoring the condition and calibration of machines on which a product is manufactured. Although quality control based on inspecting WIPs provides more accurate results (it helps to uncover minor defects, say, inaccuracies in parts alignment), there are certain limitations that hinder the method's usage:

Quality control based on WIP inspection is applicable only for discrete manufacturing. It is costly, time- and labour-intensive, as the WIPs are inspected manually. It is rarely possible to inspect every WIP, therefore, the method provides a fractional view.

The second method, based on monitoring the condition and calibration of machines, offers less differentiation in terms of scope - it provides simple binary classification "good" and "not good". However, it helps to detect bottlenecks in the manufacturing operations, identify badly tuned and/or underperforming machines, timely prevent machine damages, and more.

To monitor the quality of the production process, such parameters as equipment calibration, machine conditions (speed, vibration, etc.) and environmental conditions (temperature, humidity, etc.) are monitored to identify when they go beyond the normal thresholds. If sensor readings are approaching the thresholds that can lead to a potential product defect, a quality monitoring solution pinpoints the source of an issue, triggers an alert and recommends a mitigating action to fix or tune the machine and minimize the production of low-quality products.

Maastricht Mill, a Dutch paper producing company, has turned to IoT development to monitor the quality of produced paper. The enterprise rolled out the network of temperature and vibration sensors to monitor the condition of press rolls particularly critical for the quality of produced paper, which helped the company to minimize the amount of low-quality paper.

IoT applications for industrial asset management

Along with improving the effectiveness of manufacturing operations, the Internet of Things is applied in manufacturing to ensure proper asset usage, extend equipment service life, improve reliability, and provide the best return on assets. The IoT applications facilitating industrial asset management include:

Industrial asset tracking

Data flows through an organization like blood in the circulatory system, and each day, each hour there are a myriad...........

Inventory management

Predictive maintenance (based on condition monitoring).

Industrial asset tracking

Smart asset tracking solutions based on RFID and IoT are expected to overtake traditional, spreadsheet-based methods by 2022. By providing accurate real-time data about enterprise's assets, their statuses, locations and movements, IoT-based asset management solutions remove the tracking burden from the employees (freeing up to 18 hours of monthly working time) and eliminate errors bound to the manual methods of data input.

To enable asset tracking for manufacturing, IoT works together with RFID. Each asset – be it a magnetic locator or a crane - gets labelled with an RFID tag, which serves as an asset identifier. Each tag has a unique ID, which is linked to the data about a particular asset. Both the ID and the corresponding asset data is stored in the cloud.

The asset data may include the asset's physical parameters, cost, serial number, model, assigned employee, area of use, etc.

Once an asset, say, a crane, leaves an equipment storage yard, an RFID reader installed at the yard entrance, scans the tag attached to the crane and saves the record about the asset leaving the yard to an in-cloud database. Similarly, when the crane enters, say, a construction site, an RFID reader at the construction site entrance scans the tag and updates the data in the database. Logging such data throughout the asset's journey allows technicians to see the movements of the assets.

Along with that, GPS tracking can be used to state the location of the movable assets, for instance, machines used in construction. For movable items, asset tracking solutions are also used to calculate utilization. For instance, seeing for how long each movable (say, a bulldozer) is in use, technicians can pinpoint idling or underused machines and schedule preventive maintenance.

Construction company VerHalen Inc., for instance, turned to IoT development to implement a smart asset management solution. Now the employees can use a mobile app to see where all their assets are located. Company's managers can see how many tools and pieces of equipment are at a jobsite and who operates them. With real-time data on the tools' usage and location, the enterprise has achieved a higher level of asset visibility and accountability, as well as saved its employees vast amounts of time previously spent on manual tracking and searching for the tools.

Enterprise inventory management

IoT-driven inventory management solutions help manufacturers automate inventory tracking and reporting, ensure constant visibility into the statuses and locations of individual inventory items, and optimize lead time (the time between an inventory order and its delivery). Due to these improvements, smart inventory management solutions are reported to save 20% to 50% of an enterprise' inventory carrying costs.

Inventory management solutions applied in the manufacturing settings are based on IoT and RFID technologies. Each inventory item gets labelled with a passive RFID tag. Each tag has a unique ID that carries the data about the item the tag is attached to. To fetch the data from the tags, RFID readers are used. A reader catches tags' IDs and relays them to the cloud for storing and processing. To establish the location and the movements of the scanned tags, along with the tags' IDs, the data about the location of the RFID reader and the time of the reading are relayed to the cloud. The cloud pinpoints the location and the status of each item, visualizes the findings and displays them to the users.

Sekisui Alveo AG, a leading manufacturer of high-performance polyolefin foam materials implemented an inventory management solution based on RFID and IIoT. As the company produces finished foam products, they are labelled with RFID-tags. This makes it possible to view inventory levels in real-time, locate specific inventory items and automate inventory tracking processes that were previously handled manually.

Predictive maintenance, condition monitoring

According to Deloitte, predictive maintenance solutions based on the Industrial IoT are expected to reduce factory equipment maintenance costs by 40% and generate the economic value of $630 billion annually by 2025. The solution leads the IoT adoption – 55% of businesses are at least piloting predictive maintenance projects. This is how it is carried out from the technological perspective.

Predictive maintenance relies on the insights gained with continuous equipment condition monitoring. A piece of equipment gets sensors, which collect data on a wide range of parameters determining its health and performance, e.g. temperature, pressure, vibration frequency, etc.

Once collected, the real-time data from multiple sensors is transmitted to the cloud, where sensor readings are combined with metadata (equipment's model, configuration, operational settings, etc.), equipment usage history, and maintenance data fetched from ERP, maintenance systems and other sources. The whole of data is analysed, visualized, and presented to shop floor workers on a dashboard or in a mobile app. However, mere reporting and visualization is still far from prediction. To enable prediction, the combined data set is run through machine learning algorithms to pinpoint abnormal patterns that may lead to equipment failures.

Data scientists use the recognized data patterns as the basis for creating predictive models. The models are trained, tested, and then used to identify whether any incipient problems take place, predict when a machine is likely to fail, pinpoint operating conditions and machine usage patterns that lead to failures, etc.

For instance, machine's condition parameters (e.g., temperature, vibration, etc.), operating parameters (e.g., speed, pressure, etc.), and environmental parameters (e.g., humidity, temperature, etc.) are within normal thresholds. However, combining these parameters and analysing the joined data set against predictive models helps to reveal that the combination of parameters normal when taken separately can cause, say, a machine's engine failure. Once a potential failure is identified, the predictive maintenance solution sends a notification to the maintenance specialists, notifying them of potential degradation and recommends a mitigating action.

Data flows through an organization like blood in the circulatory system, and each day, each hour there are a myriad...........

Chapter two

Internet of Things in Healthcare

Nigeria is faced with enormous challenges with Health care, with presence of Health centres in the Local governments nationwide, health care delivery system is a mirage. Technology will aid its improvement and availability of medical care at the grass roots. Though we are looking beyond steaming and data collection, we are aware that there is a shortfall of medical personnel compared to our population , other issues that we are already used to is the lack of infrastructure , drugs , vaccines etc. our interest is processes of taking medical attention to our citizens no matter where they reside , IOT will bridge the gap.

Medical diagnostic consumes a large part of hospital bills. Technology can move the routines of medical checks from a hospital (hospital-centric) to the patient's home (home-centric). Apart from cost incurred by patients , it consumes a lot of time of the few available doctors , IOT will handle this very effectively thereby making it easy for diagnosis to be carried out without delay.

Real-time monitoring via connected devices can save lives in event of a medical emergency like heart failure, diabetes, asthma attacks, etc. With real-time monitoring of the condition in place by means of a smart medical device connected to a smartphone app, connected devices can collect medical and other required health data and use the data connection of the smartphone to transfer collected information to a physician.

This implies that Mobile Application is connected to devices in the hospitals, an upgrade from analogue to digital equipment's that can carry out tests like ECG, blood pressure, oxygen and blood sugar levels, weight. Patient connect to these devices over the internet collect various data and stored on servers of the clinic or to remove complexities of managing such IT resources, storing the data on the cloud won't be a bad idea. Physician have access to information provided by the device and the patient in question can be attended to.

Though I agree that we might not have a robust technology infrastructure to drive this initiative, the Telco's have to rise to this challenge, mobile phones ought to have positive impact on lives apart from just making a phone call. Provision of Internet connectivity on these phones will make it easy for access to such proposed services by patients across the country. The internet services must be robust and cost effective, usage will improve when the sole aim is to use it to access various devices over the internet.

Research has shown that patients spend more time at the hospitals carrying out diagnosis before doctors attend to them. A study in united states indicate that there is a 50% reduction in 30-day readmission rate because of remote patient monitoring on heart failure patients.

IoT can automate patient care workflow with the help healthcare mobility solution and other new technologies, and next-gen healthcare facilities. IoT in healthcare enables interoperability, machine-to-machine communication, information exchange, and data movement that makes healthcare service delivery effective. Connectivity protocols: Bluetooth LE, Wi-Fi, Z-wave, ZigBee, and other modern protocols, healthcare personnel can change the way they spot illness and ailments in patients and can also innovate revolutionary ways of treatment.

Consequently, technology-driven setup brings down the cost, by cutting down unnecessary visits, utilizing better quality resources, and improving the allocation and planning.

Nigeria needs no fewer than 237,000 medical doctors to meet World Health Organisation (WHO) standard, a professor of medicine and chairman, Association of Colleges of Medicine of Nigeria, Folashade Ogunsola, has said.

("**Nigeria needs 237,000 medical doctors but has only 35,000**", Premium Times, November 2, 2015 ,)

What IOT promises us is the ability of collecting medical data with ease and the physician have access , reviews and treats the patient. Our reference indicates that we don't have enough doctors to match our population and at this point Artificial intelligence can be used to take care of this deficiency in manpower , this implies that the mobile APP can be developed, this picks up the data from the cloud for the patient in question , the APP attends to the patient. It is not out of place to have these systems run on a server of a medical centre and have a dedicated doctor validate the decision of the e-doctor before prescriptions are made. The APP should be developed in 3 Major Languages and Pidgin English to ensure the population in the rural areas have access to this Application.

This not only guarantees quality medical care but ensuring the Gap is bridged , other school of thought will feel this could be strenuous for a medical personnel to vet the e-doctor at each time a patient makes use of this service, this can be regarded as a pilot so as to ensure that the e-doctor is not underperforming with respect to patient's use of the facility.

Ministry of Health should come out with a framework that ensures that the e-doctor App is introduced, IOT initiatives implemented to ease the challenges posed by diagnosis. Telco's should ensure that internet services are robust and it's interesting that a Telco giant plans to upgrade it's network from 4G to 5G , this will rub on quest for IOT and Artificial intelligence in most endeavours of life.

In event of an emergency, patients can contact a doctor who is many kilometres away with a smart mobile app. With mobility solutions in healthcare, the medics can instantly check the patients and identify the ailments on-the-go. Also, numerous healthcare delivery chains that are forecasting to build machines that can distribute drugs based on patient's prescription and ailment-related data available via linked devices. IoT will Improve the patient's care in hospital. This in turn, will cut on people's expanse on healthcare

IoT for healthcare can also be used for research purposes. It's because IoT enables us to collect a massive amount of data about the patient's illness which would have taken many years if we collected it manually.

This data thus collected can be used for statistical study that would support the medical research. Thus, IoT don't only saves time but also our money which would go in the research. Thus, IoT has a great impact in the field of medical research. It enables the introduction of bigger and better medical treatments. IoT is used in a variety of devices that enhance the quality of the healthcare services received by the patients. Even the existing devices are now being updated by IoT by simply using embedding chips of a smart devices. This chip enhances the assistance and care that a patient requires.

Obviously there are enormous challenges with this initiative , One of the most significant threats that IoT poses is of data security & privacy. IoT devices capture and transmit data in real-time. However, most of the IoT devices lack data protocols and standards. In addition to that, there is significant ambiguity regarding data ownership regulation. All these factors make the data highly susceptible to cybercriminals who can hack into the system and compromise Personal Health Information (PHI) of both patients as well as doctors. Cybercriminals can misuse patient's data to create fake IDs to buy drugs and medical equipment which they can sell later.

Integration of multiple devices also causes hindrance in the implementation of IoT in the healthcare sector. The reason for this hindrance is that device manufacturers haven't reached a consensus regarding communication protocols and standard. So, even if the variety of devices are connected; the difference in their communication protocol complicates and hinders the process of data aggregation. This non-uniformity of the connected device's protocols slows down the whole process and reduces the scope of scalability of IoT in healthcare.

Surprised to see cost considerations in the challenge sections? I know most of you would be; but the bottom line is: IoT has not made the healthcare facilitates affordable to the common man yet.

The boom in the Healthcare costs is a worrying sign for everybody especially the developed countries. The situation is such that it gave rise to "Medical Tourism" in which patients with critical conditions access healthcare facilities of the developing nations which costs them as less as one-tenth. IoT in healthcare as a concept is a fascinating and promising idea.

Data flows through an organization like blood in the circulatory system, and each day, each hour there are a myriad...........

However, it hasn't solved the cost considerations as of now. To successfully implement IoT app development and to gain its total optimization the stakeholders must make it cost effective otherwise it will always remain out of everyone's reach except the people from the high class. The rise of IoT is exciting for everybody due to its different scope of use in various sectors. In Healthcare it has several applications. IoT in healthcare helps in:

- Reducing emergency room wait time
- Tracking patients, staff, and inventory
- Enhancing drug management
- Ensuring availability of critical hardware

IOT applied to Health care is achievable in Nigeria ,most of the discussions in this chapter might look abstract and to many of us unachievable but I have the firm believe that the stakeholders have to make it work , Government remains the Piper with frameworks , reduced import duties of devices , Nigeria Medical association input will be needed for Software

Data flows through an organization like blood in the circulatory system, and each day, each hour there are a myriad............

Development outfits to knit an application that will connect to these devices , collect patients data for onward transmission to the cloud for doctors review and consequently patient's treatment.

Chapter Three

IOT in Banking and Finance

The Central bank of Nigeria, Apex bank that provides direction to financial institutions with respect to technologies have not really provided any framework on IOT with respect to banks in Nigeria. Most financial institution have taken the bull by the horn by providing cutting edge technologies that has added enormous value to services rendered.

IoT is the interconnection of uniquely identifiable embedded computing devices within the existing Internet infrastructure. IoT is expected to offer advanced connectivity of devices, systems, and services that goes beyond machine-to-machine (M2M) communications and covers a variety of protocols, domains, and applications. In the financial services space, the interconnection of these embedded devices is expected to usher in automation in several legacy processes. As IoT led digitization begins to take root, new business models and products are emerging. This is opening up new frontiers of innovation that can potentially reshape customer experiences, and throw up clear winners or losers in the financial services sector.

IoT has the potential to impact traditional business processes in banking such as KYC, lending, collateral management, trade finance, payments, PFM, and insurance. Coupled with other emerging technologies, such as digital identity and smart contacts, IoT can create new P2P business models that have the potential to disrupt banking in a few areas. Listed below are 12 use cases that may be adopted in banking in a time span ranging from near-term to long-term.

As more devices acquire digital interfaces, the term "mobile" or "digital" banking will acquire new meaning and customers will be able to access their bank accounts from practically any "thing" that has a digital interface – for instance, from entertainment systems in autonomous cars or planes.

Banks will be aware of the context of the channel and can provide appropriate contextualized service or advice enriching the interaction experience. Biometrics – voice or touch – can simplify account access in these new "anywhere" digital channels. Processes requiring physical signatures could use "Wet Ink" technology, i.e. The customer can remotely sign through any touch screen device and the signature can be cloned onto physical paper with "Wet Ink". This will eliminate barriers associated with in-person, paper-based transactions and enable clients to conduct business even when they cannot be physically present.

Real-time monitoring of wear and tear of assets as well as metrics like asset usage and idle time could provide important data points for pricing of leased assets. This could lead to introduction of a new daily leasing model for a wide variety of digitally enabled assets –

effectively turning even traditional products into services. Terms of leasing could be simplified and automated as the bank wields greater control over the leased asset. For instance, in case of contract termination or default, the leased asset could be locked or disabled remotely by the bank.

IoT technology can enable banks to have better control over a customer's mortgaged assets, such as cars, and monitor their health. In such a scenario, a retail or SME customer could possibly raise short-term small finance by offering manufacturing machinery, cars, or expensive home appliances as collateral. The request for financing as well as the transfer of ownership could be automatic and completely digital. Enabled by digital identity for people as well as things, the transfer of ownership of an asset can be achieved in a matter of seconds. The bank can then issue the loan immediately and monitor the collateral status in real-time without the need to

Data flows through an organization like blood in the circulatory system, and each day, each hour there are a myriad............

take physical custody of the asset. The bank can remotely disable or enable the machine/motor anytime based on defined business rules. For instance, in case loan EMIs are not paid, the engine could be disabled. The quality of the collateral can also be monitored in near real-time.

When moving on to payments, integration of IoT and payment functionality will lead to greater number of payment endpoints. Beyond the clichéd milk ordering refrigerator, we are already starting to see the beginning of the use of connected devices and wearables, for instance, payment through Apple Watch or the fitness band Jawbone. When machines are able to perform transactions with machines in real-time on a marginal cost basis, the traditional concept of payments will become obsolete in many use cases as transactions become automated and integrated into other services – virtually any "thing" could include an automated payment experience. Though the IoT raises certain security concerns, personal biometrics and digital identities could potentially increase security in payments, if done right. Eventually the opportunity extends not only to the end user, for whom automated payments will lead to greater convenience and smarter transactions, but to banks, payments companies, retailers, and technology manufacturers.

Tracking of high value goods delivery using RFID is already reality in the trade finance space. IoT will accelerate this to include fine-grained tracking of the asset, for instance, monitoring temperature of the container for shipments involving temperature sensitive goods such as pharmaceuticals and medicinal molecules. Alerts could be triggered if there is a chance of spoilage during the shipment process – say one of the parameters being monitored goes out of bounds. These implementations can result in risk mitigation and more informed decision making at banks for scenarios involving trade finance.

Data flows through an organization like blood in the circulatory system, and each day, each hour there are a myriad...........

Banks crave holistic insights into customers' financial behaviour. Having this information during customer onboarding can help them profile the customer correctly and cross-sell relevant products. However, information available at the bank's disposal at this stage is scarce and does not provide a comprehensive view of the customer's financial behaviour. In a world where all the customer's devices are linked together with the customer's digital identity, having access to the customer's unique digital footprint might help uncover usage patterns of different devices and provide insights into financial behaviour as well. People already use their Facebook / Gmail id to login to different Internet sites; this might be extended in the future to have a blockchain-based unique digital signature which is used for most transactions. This universal blockchain-based digital identity may also help with KYC processes in the future. Knowing about the financial inclinations of the customer through the digital signature, banks can offer relevant products at the time of onboarding – for e.g. offer a co-branded credit card designed with rewards from a petrol station that the customer frequents.

Smart contracts are computer programs that facilitate, verify, or enforce the negotiation or performance of a contract. IoT, together with smart contracts and digital identity, can make payments partially or fully self-executing and self-enforcing. For instance, pay after a trial of 7 days for home appliances, or control access to a house based on timely payment of rent. This model of IoT-assisted smart contracts holds huge potential in terms of process automation and mitigation of operational risks. More importantly, this can plausibly create new product options which offer better customer experience.

Nigerian Banks invest heavily on Technology , Customers in the comfort of their homes can apply for facilities on any handheld device , the software collates information provided and consequently analyse the financial records of the customer in question and take decisions , however this is subject to volume of credit involved. Credit risk unit has the responsibility to ensure the laid down policies are followed, and the criteria is met.

Cashless policy introduced during Lamido's tenure as CBN governor has also improved payments by electronic means, though still bewildered with many infrastructural challenges. IOT is the seamless connection of devices across the institution that will bank services available to customers , ATM operation involves FEP server , Bank Application and the FEP routes to NIBBS Server when there is an interbank payments , this is a classical example of IOT and our banks should look beyond this and provide excellent service.

Account Opening can be done without a customer necessarily visiting the bank, can be done from the comfort of their homes, today most banks have initiated this but restricted to only savings account for now.

Investment in Treasury bills is also automated, customers don't need to be stressed, just an APP you can invest in Treasury bills from the comfort of your home using a mobile phone.

Banking has undergone series of transformation compared to what was obtainable in the 80's , these are as a result of improvement of processes with the aid of a mobile phone and most of us cannot recall when last we stepped into the banking hall for transactions , it's either we carryout transfers on our phones, ATM machines , Kiosks etc.

The Telco's remain the main provider of services that would ensure seamless connectivity for the users , most of the Telco's are scrambling for mobile money services , ensuring subscribers have banks in their pockets and this will bring these services into reality apart from depending solely on calls , Telco's can double their income by a little creativity.

Chapter Four

IOT in Agriculture

Nigeria is evolving in food production and other initiatives connected to agriculture, the smartest way to go is to embrace IOT for enhanced performance, it is pertinent to note that the rural population are the most engaged in farming , technology can be deployed to their localities and as we have indicated in the last two chapters , Telco's must be involved because the story here is to bring devices together with their services and ensure there is a handshake.

Smart farming based on IoT technologies will enable growers and farmers to reduce waste and enhance productivity ranging from the quantity of fertilizer utilized to the number of journeys the farm vehicles have made. So what is smart farming? Smart farming is a capital-intensive and hi-tech system of growing food cleanly and sustainable for the masses. It is the application of modern ICT (Information and Communication Technologies) into agriculture.

In IoT-based smart farming, a system is built for monitoring the crop field with the help of sensors (light, humidity, temperature, soil moisture, etc.) and automating the irrigation system. The farmers can monitor the field conditions from anywhere. IoT-based smart farming is highly efficient when compared with the conventional approach. The applications of IoT-based smart farming not only target conventional, large farming operations, but could also be new levers to uplift other growing or common trends in agricultural like organic farming, family farming (complex or small spaces, particular cattle and/or cultures, preservation of particular or high quality varieties etc.), and enhance highly transparent farming.

In terms of environmental issues, IoT-based smart farming can provide great benefits including more efficient water usage, or optimization of inputs and treatments. Now, let's discuss the major applications of IoT-based smart farming that are revolutionizing agriculture.

precision farming can be thought of as anything that makes the farming practice more controlled and accurate when it comes to raising livestock and growing of crops. In this approach of farm management, a key component is the use of IT and various items like sensors, control systems, robotics, autonomous vehicles, automated hardware, variable rate technology, and so on.

The adoption of access to high-speed internet, mobile devices, and reliable, low-cost satellites (for imagery and positioning) by the manufacturer are few key technologies characterizing the precision agriculture trend. Precision agriculture is one of the most famous applications of IoT in the agricultural sector and numerous organizations are leveraging this technique around the world.

IOT aides VRI optimization, soil moisture probes, virtual optimizer PRO, and so on. VRI (Variable Rate Irrigation) optimization maximizes profitability on irrigated crop fields with topography or soil variability, improve yields, and increases water use efficiency. The soil moisture probe technology provides complete in-season local agronomy support, and recommendations to optimize water use efficiency. The virtual optimizer PRO combines various technologies for water management into one central, cloud based, and powerful location designed for consultants and growers to take advantage of the benefits in precision irrigation via a simplified interface.

Technology has changed over time and agricultural drones are a very good example of this. Today, agriculture is one of the major industries to incorporate drones. Drones are being used in agriculture in order to enhance various agricultural practices. The ways ground-based and aerial based drones are being used in agriculture are crop health assessment, irrigation, crop monitoring, crop spraying, planting, and soil and field analysis. The major benefits of using drones include crop health imaging, integrated GIS mapping, ease of use, saves time, and the potential to increase yields. With strategy and planning based on real-time data collection and processing, the drone technology will give a high-tech makeover to the agriculture industry.

Drones could be used for gathering valuable data via a series of sensors that are used for imaging, mapping, and surveying of agricultural land. These drones perform in-flight monitoring and observations. The farmers enter the details of what field to survey, and select an altitude or ground resolution. From the drone data, we can draw insights regarding plant health indices, plant counting and yield prediction, plant height measurement, canopy cover mapping, field water posing mapping, scouting reports, stockpile measuring, chlorophyll measurement, nitrogen content in wheat, drainage mapping, weed pressure mapping, and so on. The drone collects multispectral, thermal, and visual imagery during the flight and then lands in the same location it took off.

Large farm owners can utilize wireless IoT applications to collect data regarding the location, well-being, and health of their cattle. This information helps them in identifying animals that are sick so they can be separated from the herd, thereby preventing the spread of disease. It also lowers labour costs as ranchers can locate their cattle with the help of IoT based sensors. . One of the solutions helps the cattle owners observe cows that are pregnant and about to give birth. From the heifer, a sensor powered by battery is expelled when its water breaks. This sends an information to the herd manager or the rancher. In the time that is spent with heifers that are giving birth, the sensor enables farmers to be more focused.

Greenhouse farming is a methodology that helps in enhancing the yield of vegetables, fruits, crops etc. Greenhouses control the

Data flows through an organization like blood in the circulatory system, and each day, each hour there are a myriad...........

environmental parameters through manual intervention or a proportional control mechanism. As manual intervention results in production loss, energy loss, and labor cost, these methods are less effective. A smart greenhouse can be designed with the help of IoT; this design intelligently monitors as well as controls the climate, eliminating the need for manual intervention.

For controlling the environment in a smart greenhouse, different sensors that measure the environmental parameters according to the plant requirement are used. We can create a cloud server for remotely accessing the system when it is connected using IoT. This eliminates the need for constant manual monitoring. Inside the greenhouse, the cloud server also enables data processing and applies a control action. This design provides cost-effective and optimal solutions to the farmers with minimal manual intervention.

greenhouses by using solar powered IoT sensors. With these sensors, the greenhouse state and water consumption can be monitored via SMS alerts to the farmer with an online portal. Automatic Irrigation is carried out in these greenhouses. The IoT sensors in the greenhouse provide information on the light levels, pressure, humidity, and temperature. These sensors can control the actuators automatically to open a window, turn on lights, control a heater, turn on a mister or turn on a fan, all controlled through a Wi-Fi signal.

IOT service providers deploy these technologies mentioned in this chapter, it makes farm management effective , eliminate waste, losses etc. , note that a large poultry farm can be managed effectively making it possible to detect when there is a disease outbreak , let us assume the farm has 10,000 birds , IOT initiative will help to ensure that information is released to the farmer via SMS for prompt and immediate action.

Chapter Five

IOT in Public sector

We have looked at sectors of the economy and it will be an error under the sun to exclude the public sector , I'm aware of government initiative on ease of doing business in Nigeria that is bound at attracting foreign investments and this transcends to a great economy , vibrant market.

IOT can propel this phenomenon, collocation of servers of CAC, FIRS , other relevant agencies that are involved. The implication is that with your handheld device business registration can be consummated with ease.

Have we wondered why budgets are delayed by concerned MDA, Agencies and parastatals? The answer is not farfetched because it is done manually and there is no smart means of collecting data that would serve as a guide. A simple centralized application will make the process simple and removing ambiguity associated with paperwork. I can imagine Mr president carrying bulky paper to the house of senate for deliberation and approval. The process is cumbersome automating it will not improve quick delivery but also sped in terms of its defence by parastatals at the red chambers.

IOT comes into play for Asset management, you have an idea if it's fully depreciated and most importantly whether it can be deployed against the next budget in case approval is not gotten in the preceding year.

''The technology is in its infancy in the public sector, at both the federal and the local levels. "The Internet of Things is super-promising for local and state governments, but because it's an emerging technology, it can be expensive and it is relatively untested," New explained. "That creates a high level of perceived risk."

(Practical Uses of the Internet of Things in Government Are Everywhere, Government Technology, TAM HARBERT FEBRUARY 2017)

Data flows through an organization like blood in the circulatory system, and each day, each hour there are a myriad...........

Though we might not dispute the fact that IOT might be at its infancy in most countries but the initiative would guide the government in making adequate plans to improve infrastructures since data is available for decision making rather than wait till there is a collapse before action is taken. Management of Toll gate collections can be audited with an IOT that provides information on daily basis of number of vehicles that had visited the toll gate.

This is an area that can help us manage Amenities in urban and rural areas and ensure it is not over stretched by availing available data to appropriate constituted authorities for decisions to be taken.

IOT is a very important concept that must be embraced by all the sectors of the economy, Service providers are not existing for now probably because it's a new kind of technology that promises to impact lives positively and remove ambiguities usually experienced. The stakeholders

Data flows through an organization like blood in the circulatory system, and each day, each hour there are a myriad...........

are to take positions and make it a success in Nigeria.

www.ingramcontent.com/pod-product-compliance
Lightning Source LLC
Chambersburg PA
CBHW031248050326

40690CB00007B/999